Yours for Justice, Ida B. Wells

The Daring Life of a Crusading Journalist

In memory of Mrs. Fannie Lee Chaney
and Dr. Carolyn Goodman

—*P. D.*

For Odetta,
with profound admiration

—*S. A.*

Published by
PEACHTREE PUBLISHERS
1700 Chattahoochee Avenue
Atlanta, Georgia 30318-2112
www.peachtree-online.com

Text © 2008 by Philip Dray
Illustrations © 2008 by Stephen Alcorn

Book and cover design by Stephen Alcorn
and Loraine M. Joyner

Illustrations created as giclee prints of original drawings on archival vellum and hand-tinted
in watercolor. Text typeset in Baskerville Infant; titles typeset in International Typeface
Corporation's Caxton; quotation insets typeset in Monotype Imaging's Lucida Calligraphy.

Photos on pages 42 and 43 courtesy of the University of Chicago Library, Special Collections
Research Center; illustration on page 44 courtesy of North Wind Picture Archives;
photo on page 45 courtesy of the Library of Congress

Printed in Singapore
10 9 8 7 6 5 4 3 2 1
First Edition

Library of Congress Cataloging-in-Publication Data
Dray, Philip.
Yours for justice, Ida B. Wells : the daring life of a crusading journalist /
written by Philip Dray ; illustrated by Stephen Alcorn. — 1st ed.
p. cm.
Includes bibliographical references.
ISBN-13: 978-1-56145-417-4
ISBN-10: 1-56145-417-6
1. Wells-Barnett, Ida B., 1862-1931—Juvenile literature. 2. African American women civil
rights workers—Biography—Juvenile literature. 3. Civil rights workers—United States—
Biography—Juvenile literature. 4. African American women educators
—Biography—Juvenile literature. 5. African American women journalists—Biography
—Juvenile literature. 6. United States—Race relations—Juvenile literature. 7. African
Americans—Civil rights—History—Juvenile literature. 8. African Americans—Social
conditions—To 1964—Juvenile literature. 9. Lynching—United States—History
—Juvenile literature. I. Alcorn, Stephen. II. Title.

E185.97.W55D73 2007
323.092—dc22
[B]
2007004016

Yours for Justice, Ida B. Wells

The Daring Life of a Crusading Journalist

Philip Dray

Illustrated by
Stephen Alcorn

PEACHTREE
ATLANTA

*I*DA B. WELLS was born a slave in Holly Springs, Mississippi, in 1862. The Civil War had started the year before, and sometimes her town was filled with the terrible sounds of battle.

For the Wells family, though, work went on much as it had before the war.

Jim and Lizzie Wells were slaves who belonged to a white man named Mr. Bolling. Jim was a carpenter in Mr. Bolling's shop, and Lizzie served as the family's cook. The Wells were treated better than many slaves. Mr. Bolling did not whip or beat them for mistakes, and he gave them enough food and clothing. But his slaves were still his property. Mr. Bolling could even choose to sell baby Ida away from her family if he wanted. When Jim and Lizzie heard rumors that there were people working to end slavery, they treasured the hope that they—and especially Ida—might one day be free.

When Ida was nearly three years old, the Civil War ended. Slavery was made illegal, and people like Ida and her parents were finally free.

Jim and Lizzie Wells began building a new life for themselves. Lizzie stopped working and stayed home to take care of Ida. Jim kept his carpentry job, but Mr. Bolling now paid him for his work.

Some whites thought that black people were not ready for the responsibilities of freedom, especially voting. As election time drew near, Mr. Bolling told Ida's father who to vote for. He made it clear that if Jim wanted to keep his job, he had better do what he was told.

On election day, Jim Wells proudly cast his votes for the men he thought would be best for Mississippi—not for Mr. Bolling's candidates. When he got back to the carpentry shop, his boss had locked him out to punish him!

Determined not to be defeated, Jim Wells bought some tools and started his own carpentry business. He also moved his family into a house away from Mr. Bolling. At the time Ida didn't understand why. But as she grew older, she realized that her father had refused to work for a man who would not respect his rights. Freedom was far too important to him.

Before the Civil War, many slaves like Jim and Lizzie were not allowed to learn to read and write. When Ida was old enough to attend Holly Springs's new school for blacks, her mother went with her. Once Lizzie learned enough to read her Bible, she stopped going. She needed to stay home to care for her growing family. But she made sure that her children kept at their lessons. Ida found she especially loved to read. One by one, she read every novel at her school and church libraries.

Although Ida liked going to school, she often had a hard time getting along with others, especially her teachers. Even at this early age, Ida had a mind of her own and didn't hesitate to give her opinion.

The oldest of eight children, Ida found that a strong will sometimes came in handy. She was a great help to her mother in doing household chores and in looking after her younger siblings. One of her favorite chores was reading newspapers aloud to her father and his friends at night. Reading these articles gave Ida knowledge about the world far beyond Holly Springs—and she saw how powerful the written word could be.

When Ida was sixteen, a yellow fever epidemic swept through Holly Springs. Many people in her town got the horrible disease, and to Ida's great sorrow, her parents and a baby brother died from it.

Friends and neighbors argued over who should take care of the Wells children. When Ida heard them making plans to break up her family, she couldn't remain silent. She announced that if the adults would help her find a job, she would take care of her brothers and sisters herself.

At first no one believed she could do it. But Ida would not take no for an answer. Someone suggested that she try to become a teacher in one of the smaller country schools, and Ida agreed.

Her aunt lowered the hems of Ida's dresses and taught her to put her hair up. When she saw herself in the mirror, Ida couldn't believe her eyes: she looked like a grown-up! A few weeks later, she passed the teachers' exam with high marks and began her first teaching job.

Ida quickly found that passing the exam was much easier than teaching her students.

Her schoolhouse looked more like a barn than a classroom, and it was usually very crowded. Many students were so poor they often didn't have enough to eat, and this made it hard for them to learn. To make matters worse, Ida had to teach all ages at the same time. With only a few books and supplies, her work was nearly impossible.

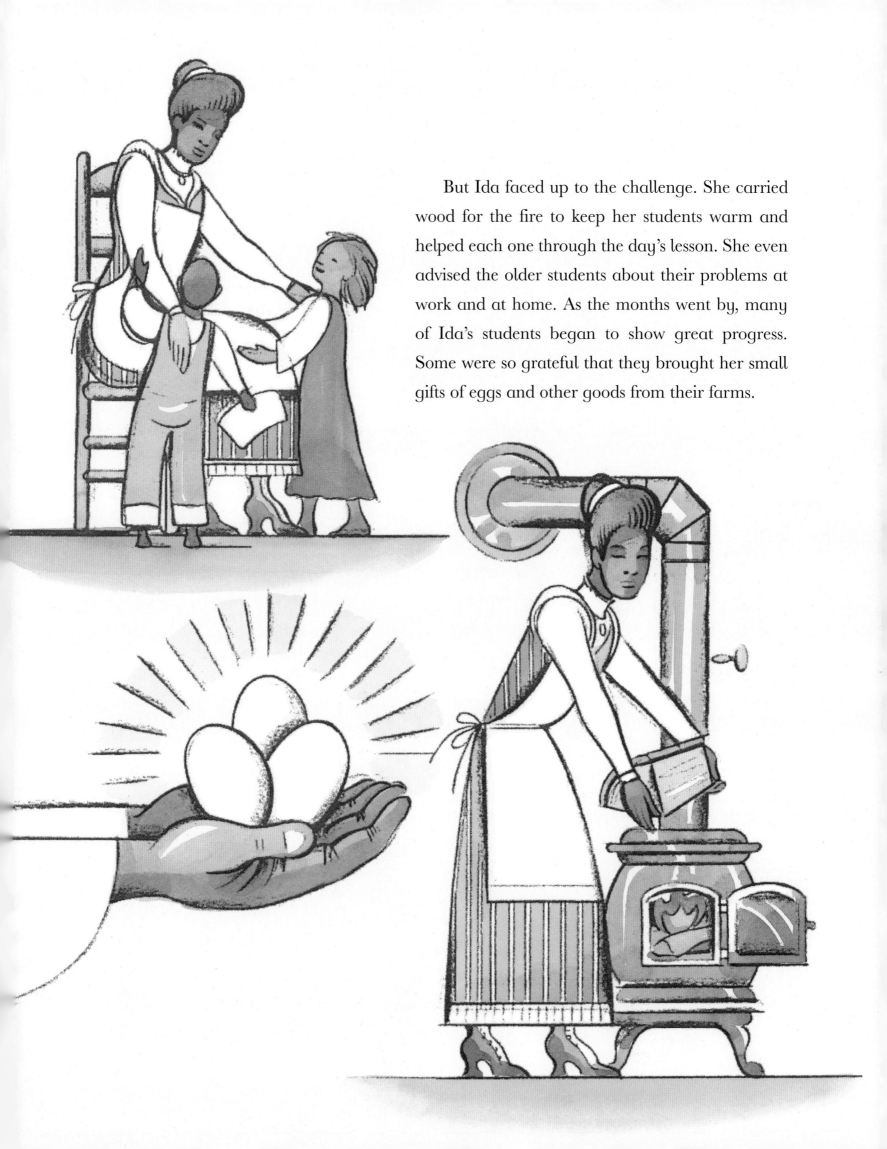

But Ida faced up to the challenge. She carried wood for the fire to keep her students warm and helped each one through the day's lesson. She even advised the older students about their problems at work and at home. As the months went by, many of Ida's students began to show great progress. Some were so grateful that they brought her small gifts of eggs and other goods from their farms.

When her brothers and sisters were older, Ida was able to take a better teaching position in Memphis, Tennessee, a bustling city of streetcars and steamboats. To Ida, it was a whole new world.

The new teaching job was difficult, but Ida was paid more money. She was able to shop for the finest dresses, gloves, and boots—and especially stylish hats. She caught the eye of more than a few young admirers, but she had too many plans to think about marriage. While other girls she knew were beginning to marry and have children, Ida dreamed of becoming an actress, a journalist, or even a novelist.

She joined a group called a lyceum. Each Friday she and other teachers met to read essays or poetry and debate their ideas. These lively meetings, Ida said, were a "breath of life to me."

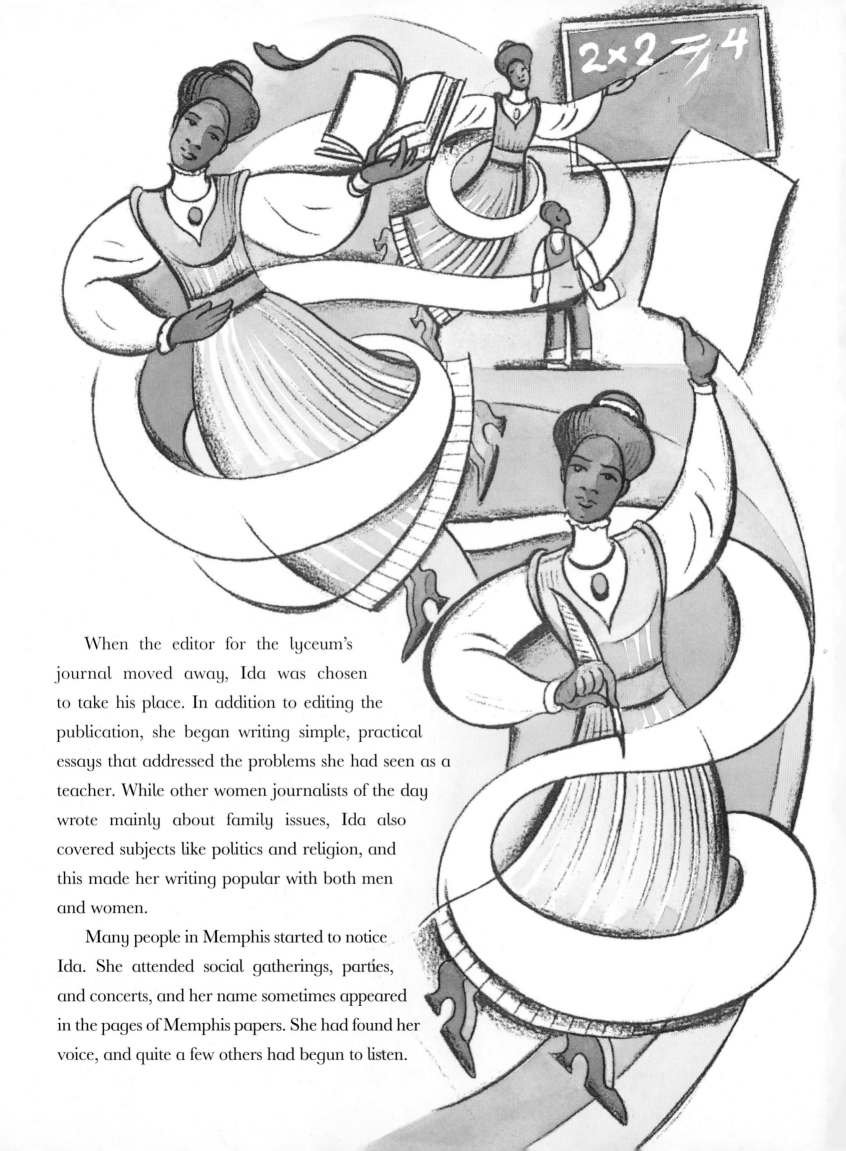

When the editor for the lyceum's journal moved away, Ida was chosen to take his place. In addition to editing the publication, she began writing simple, practical essays that addressed the problems she had seen as a teacher. While other women journalists of the day wrote mainly about family issues, Ida also covered subjects like politics and religion, and this made her writing popular with both men and women.

Many people in Memphis started to notice Ida. She attended social gatherings, parties, and concerts, and her name sometimes appeared in the pages of Memphis papers. She had found her voice, and quite a few others had begun to listen.

Sadly, Ida found plenty to speak against. Many whites still did not see blacks as equals, and they were working harder than ever to take away black people's freedoms. Some storeowners refused to sell to black customers, and they put up Whites Only signs in their windows. Certain restaurants, hotels, and even train cars were now off-limits to black customers. And new segregation laws—sometimes called Jim Crow laws—made this type of discrimination legal.

One day Ida boarded the train to her school. A few minutes into the trip, a conductor came to her seat and told her that the first-class railroad car was only for white people. He told her she had to move to a car for black people. Ida replied that she had bought a first class ticket and would remain in her seat.

Ida's response made the conductor very angry. He asked some other men to help him, and they forced Ida out of her seat. Ida was frightened, but she would not be bullied. Rather than ride in another railroad car, Ida chose to get off the train. But, like her father, she would not give up her rights without a fight.

When Ida got back to Memphis, she hired a lawyer to help her sue the railroad company. She hoped the courts would rule that the conductor and the laws that protected him were wrong. Perhaps if she won her case, it would set an example for fighting Jim Crow laws across the nation.

Months later, Ida was delighted when a white judge in Memphis ruled that the railroad would have to pay her $500. She had fought to defend her freedom and she had won!

Unfortunately, Ida's joy was short-lived. The railroad appealed the decision to the Tennessee Supreme Court, and it overturned Ida's victory. She was disappointed for her loss, but most of all Ida was heartbroken for all the black people who would continue to live under Jim Crow laws. "I had hoped for such great things from my suit for my people…," she wrote in her diary, "and just now if it were possible [I] would gather my race in my arms and fly away with them."

She had lost one battle,
but Ida looked for other ways to
fight the Jim Crow laws. An editor
of a church publication called the
Living Way asked her to write an article
about her court case against the railroad.
Her article was so successful that it was
reprinted in newspapers around the country.

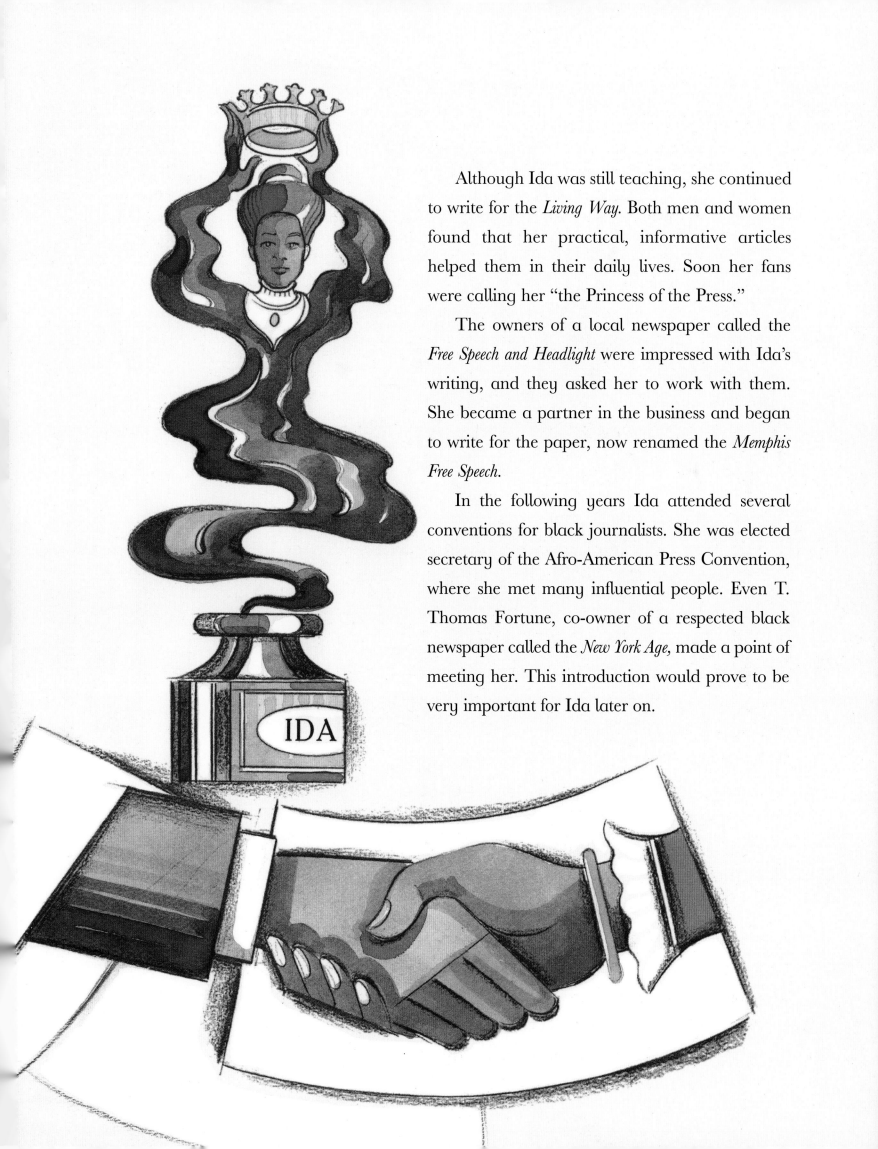

Although Ida was still teaching, she continued to write for the *Living Way.* Both men and women found that her practical, informative articles helped them in their daily lives. Soon her fans were calling her "the Princess of the Press."

The owners of a local newspaper called the *Free Speech and Headlight* were impressed with Ida's writing, and they asked her to work with them. She became a partner in the business and began to write for the paper, now renamed the *Memphis Free Speech.*

In the following years Ida attended several conventions for black journalists. She was elected secretary of the Afro-American Press Convention, where she met many influential people. Even T. Thomas Fortune, co-owner of a respected black newspaper called the *New York Age,* made a point of meeting her. This introduction would prove to be very important for Ida later on.

Ida liked writing so much that she longed to give up her teaching job. But to make a living as a journalist, she knew she would have to persuade many more people to buy the *Free Speech*. So she rode trains through Mississippi, Tennessee, and Arkansas, meeting people and urging them to read her newspaper.

Ida and J. L. Fleming, one of her business partners, came up with the unusual idea of printing the *Free Speech* on pink paper. This made the newspaper more distinctive, and even people who couldn't read immediately recognized it as the *Free Speech*.

Within a year, their hard work paid off. Subscriptions to the *Free Speech* went from 1,500 to 4,000. Ida was now able to support herself with her writing. Although newspaper work was demanding, Ida said she was "happy in the thought that our influence was helpful and that I was doing the work I loved...."

One spring day in 1892, while on a speaking tour, Ida received terrible news. Her good friend Tom Moss had been killed. Ida rushed back to Memphis at once. When she found out what had happened, she could hardly believe it.

Tom Moss and two other men ran a popular food store in Memphis called The People's Grocery. A white man who owned a store nearby became jealous of their success and let it be known that he wanted to put Tom's store out of business.

Tom knew that he and his friends could not depend on the Memphis police for protection. They would have to defend the store themselves if any trouble developed. Tensions in the neighborhood continued to rise, and one night several white men stormed The People's Grocery. Tom's friends fired their guns and the attackers fled. No white men were charged, but Tom and his friends were arrested.

Tom hoped a judge would understand that they had been trying to protect their property. But before he and his friends could make their case in court, a mob of white men took them out of the jail and murdered them. This kind of execution outside the law was known as lynching.

People from all over Memphis came to the funeral or sent flowers to show their sympathy for the men and their families. Ida did all she could to comfort Tom's wife and young daughter.

Even though many people knew who had lynched Tom Moss and his business partners, not a single person would turn in the guilty men. No one was ever punished for the murders.

Ida saw that most whites in Memphis were not willing to defend the rights of black citizens. Angry and hurt, she wrote in the *Free Speech,* "There is therefore only one thing left that we can do; save our money and leave a town which will neither protect our lives and property, nor give us a fair trial in the courts."

Hundreds of black people did just that. They fled to other places where they hoped to escape lynching and Jim Crow laws. With the *Free Speech*'s encouragement, many black residents of Memphis crossed the Mississippi River and headed west in trains, on wagons, and on foot.

Despite her advice to others, Ida stayed and protested the murder of Tom Moss and his partners. Like many Americans, she had once thought lynching was a punishment used only on the most horrible criminals. But if it could happen to Tom, she realized that other innocent people were probably being killed this way too.

Ida traveled across the country to talk with people who had seen lynching up close. She read articles in the *Chicago Tribune* and other big city newspapers. She learned that it was most often black men—like her friend Tom—who were lynched. At the heart of the problem, she realized, was the refusal of many white people to accept that black people were now free and deserved the right to a fair trial.

...cts she had gathered in hand, Ida

...r *Free Speech* readers the truth about

...gh her newspaper only reached a

...people, Ida was not discouraged.

...at if good people, white and black,

...horrors of lynching, together they

...ay to stop it.

While many of Ida's readers applauded her strong words against lynching, the articles angered some people in Memphis. When Ida was away on a trip, her business partner J. L. Fleming got word that trouble was brewing. If he didn't want to get hurt, his neighbor warned, he had better get out of town.

Later, a group of white men broke into the offices of the *Free Speech*. They smashed desks, lamps, chairs, and supplies and threw all the papers and books to the floor. The men left a note saying they would harm the owners of the newspaper if they tried to reopen it. But the mob never got the chance. Her partner had already fled, and Ida was on a train headed toward New York City. T. Thomas Fortune, the editor of the *New York Age*, had invited her to come for a visit.

Thomas met Ida at the train station. She later described the meeting in her diary.

"Well, we've been a long time getting you to New York," Thomas said, "but now you are here, I'm afraid you will have to stay."

"I can't see why that follows," Ida replied.

"Haven't you seen the morning paper?" He handed her a copy of the *New York Sun* and pointed to an article. It said that the *Free Speech* office had been destroyed! Ida was shocked and angry. She wanted to go back to Memphis and rebuild the newspaper. But where would she find the money? And how would she protect herself?

Thomas urged Ida to stay in New York and write for his paper, and he suggested that she begin with an article on lynching. The *New York Age* was one of the most popular black newspapers in America! After thinking it over, Ida happily agreed.

Ida quickly settled into her new home and began working on an article for the *Age*. She had once written, "The way to right wrongs is to turn the light of truth upon them." This was her chance to do just that.

The morning the article appeared on newsstands, Ida walked along the street, wondering what her readers would think. Would her words really make a difference?

Much to Ida's surprise, her article changed many lives. The well-known black leader Frederick Douglass called it a "revelation." For the first time, people realized that scores of innocent lives were being claimed each year by lynch mobs. Ida's article had shown lynching for what it really was: an attack on the freedom promised to all Americans.

The issue that featured Ida's article sold 10,000 copies across the nation. At least a thousand copies were sold in Memphis alone! The mob that had silenced the *Free Speech* had actually helped Ida spread the truth about lynching.

Ida had not set out to become a crusader, but the article in the *Age* made her just that. She received invitations from across the country to speak about lynching. Politicians, ministers, and other leaders wanted to know more about the problem and how they could help. And as she continued to write articles and speak out, support for her cause grew. Her *New York Age* article appeared in 1892. By her death in 1931, lynching in America had nearly come to an end.

Ida took up many other campaigns in her life-time, but none were more important than her difficult crusade against lynching. Putting an end to the practice would take decades of hard work by many courageous and dedicated people. Yet Ida's firm belief in the country she loved could never be shaken. Against every fear and doubt, her voice rang out clearly: "We submit all to...the Nation confident that, in this cause, as well as all others, 'Truth is mighty and will prevail.'"

Afterword

More About Ida

Ida B. Wells Barnett (1862-1931)

AFTER HER FIRST major article against lynching, Ida continued to write about its horrors for the *New York Age*, as well as other publications. She traveled throughout America and England, giving speeches about lynching. She also worked closely with other activists of the day, such as Frederick Douglass and W. E. B. Du Bois. In 1909, Ida helped found the National Association for the Advancement of Colored People (NAACP), a group that she hoped would promote black interests. But Ida still continued doing what she did best—publishing her ideas, speaking out against injustice, and agitating for change.

While working on one of her publications, Ida met Ferdinand L. Barnett, a newspaperman and activist who shared many of her passions. She moved to Chicago to be near him, and they were married in 1895. From that point on, Ida was usually known as Ida B. Wells-Barnett. In addition to caring for her family—two children from Ferdinand's previous marriage and four children of their own—Ida kept up her quest for social justice.

> *"What is or should be a woman? ...A strong, bright presence with a sense of her mission on earth and a desire to fill it."*
>
> – Ida B. Wells, *Woman's Mission*

In Chicago, Ida helped stop the segregation of the city's public schools, worked to integrate women's clubs in the region, and founded an organization to help black men and boys, similar to the YMCA (Young Men's Christian Association). She was instrumental in opening Chicago's first kindergarten for black children.

Ida also joined the national fight for women's suffrage. She started a black women's suffrage club in the Chicago area and worked with Susan B. Anthony and other leaders as they struggled to

> *"I thought it was right to strike a blow against a glaring evil and I did not regret it."*
>
> – Ida B. Wells, *Crusade for Justice*

gain voting rights for women. Once when she was asked to march in a separate colored section at a suffrage march, Ida refused. Instead, she single-handedly integrated the march.

Ida never gave up her battle against lynching, but as her efforts began to pay off, she found more ways to fight prejudice. She met with Woodrow Wilson, the president of the United States, to plead for the desegregation of his administration. In the 1920s, she wrote about the race riots in Illinois and Arkansas. Her writings on the riot in Arkansas helped to free twelve men who had been arrested unjustly.

Ida with her children Charles, Herman, Ida Jr., and Alfreda in 1909

When Ida was in her sixties, she became one of the first black women in the country to run for a seat in the Illinois state senate. Although she lost the election, Ida took advantage of the public attention to champion the causes of freedom and justice she had fought for all her life. On March 21, 1931, Ida fell ill with a kidney disease. She died a few days later.

The signature Ida used in promoting her writing and lectures now stands as a poignant summary of her life:

Yours for justice, Ida B. Wells.

TIMELINE

1861	American Civil War begins.
1862	Ida Wells is born.
1863	Emancipation Proclamation grants freedom to slaves.
1865	Civil War ends. New Black Codes are passed by states to restrict blacks' freedoms.
1868	14th Amendment gives freed slaves the right of citizenship.
1870	15th Amendment grants freed slaves the right to vote.
1876	First "Jim Crow" laws appear.
1878	Ida's parents die, and Ida takes over the care of her younger siblings.
1882	Ida moves to Memphis.
1884	Ida sues Chesapeake & Ohio Railroad.
1885	185 lynchings in America
1889	Ida becomes editor of the *Memphis Free Speech*.
1892	After the murder of Tom Moss, Ida begins a campaign against lynching. Her articles appear in the *New York Age* and other papers. She publishes SOUTHERN HORRORS: LYNCH LAW IN ALL ITS PHASES.
1893	Ida publishes THE REASON WHY THE COLORED AMERICAN IS NOT IN THE WORLD'S COLUMBIAN EXPOSITION: THE AFRO-AMERICAN'S CONTRIBUTION TO COLUMBIAN LITERATURE. She begins tours of England and Scotland, rousing support against lynching in America.
1895	179 lynchings in America
1895	Ida marries Chicago attorney and activist Ferdinand L. Barnett. She becomes the editor of Barnett's newspaper, *The Conservator*. Ida publishes A RED RECORD: TABULATED STATISTICS AND ALLEGED CAUSES OF LYNCHING IN THE UNITED STATES, 1892-1893-1894.

TIMELINE CONTINUED ON NEXT SPREAD

More About Lynching

BY DEFINITION, a lynching occurs any-time people go outside the law to punish a person for an alleged crime. Early in America's history, people who lived in rural areas or on the frontier often used lynching to seek justice when no legal authorities could be found. If a crime was committed, men would organize a mob to hunt down the accused person and then, without a proper trial, inflict punishment such as whipping, or tar and feathering.

After the Civil War, however, lynching became more sinister. Although black slaves like Ida were granted freedom, many whites worked to take away their new rights. Some even resorted to violence. These people used lynching to make black citizens

> "The people must know before they can act, and there is no educator to compare with the press."
>
> —Ida B. Wells, *Southern Horrors*

too afraid to vote, to run for political office, or to demand to be treated as equals. Lynch mobs often ripped their victims from homes or jail cells, tortured them, and then hanged them or burned them alive. A number of white journalists and politicians praised lynching as a form of swift justice, and they convinced many others that lynching, though illegal, was necessary to keep black people in their place.

Since lynching was condoned by so many, it became nearly impossible to punish anyone involved, and the practice grew more widespread. By the early 1890s, a black person was lynched almost every other day in America.

Political cartoon depicting the burning of Lady Liberty by "Judge Lynch"

When Ida spoke out against lynching, she knew she was taking a great risk, exposing herself as a target for lynchers. Yet the loss of her friend Tom Moss awakened in her a deep passion about the subject, and her writing and speeches inspired many around the country. Other journalists, activists, and law-makers gradually learned the truth about lynching too, and they took action. As they won the battle for public opinion, lynching began to seem unthinkable

Silent parade in New York City protesting lynching—1917

to most Americans. In 1898, a total of 158 lynchings were reported in the United States. In 1927, only 16 lynchings occurred. In 1952, twenty-one years after Ida's death, America recorded its first year without a lynching.

The desire of some whites to oppress blacks—a root cause of lynching—continued to find expression in practices such as race riots, voter fraud, and segregation. These problems went largely unchecked until the civil rights movement of the 1950s and 1960s, when activists like Dr. Martin Luther King Jr. and Rosa Parks brought new energy and dedication to the fight for social justice. Their efforts would further realize many of the hopes once held by a strong-willed girl from Holly Springs who set out against great odds to speak the truth clearly.

Note: Lynching statistics provided by the Tuskegee Institute.

Bibliography

In researching and writing YOURS FOR JUSTICE, IDA B. WELLS, I consulted many books. The following sources were particularly useful:

DeCosta-Willis, Miriam, ed. THE MEMPHIS DIARY OF IDA B. WELLS. Beacon Press.

Duster, Alfreda M., ed. CRUSADE FOR JUSTICE: THE AUTOBIOGRAPHY OF IDA B. WELLS. University of Chicago Press.

Harris, Trudier, comp. SELECTED WORKS OF IDA B. WELLS-BARNETT. Oxford University Press.

McMurry, Linda O. TO KEEP THE WATERS TROUBLED: THE LIFE OF IDA B. WELLS. Oxford University Press.

Royster, Jacqueline Jones. SOUTHERN HORRORS AND OTHER WRITINGS: THE ANTI-LYNCHING CAMPAIGN OF IDA B. WELLS, 1892–1900. Bedford Books.

Thompson, Mildred I. IDA B. WELLS-BARNETT, AN EXPLORATORY STUDY OF AN AMERICAN BLACK WOMAN, 1893–1930. Carlson Publishing.

Fradin, Dennis Brindell and **Judith Bloom Fradin**. IDA B. WELLS: MOTHER OF THE CIVIL RIGHTS MOVEMENT. Clarion Books.

> *"When this conscience wakes and speaks out in thunder tones, as it must, it will need facts to use as a weapon against injustice, barbarism and wrong. It is for this reason that I carefully compile, print and send forth these facts."*
>
> —Ida B. Wells, *Mob Rule in New Orleans*

Further reading on Ida B. Wells-Barnett for young readers:

Ages 4–8

Freedman, Suzanne. IDA B. WELLS-BARNETT AND THE ANTI-LYNCHING CRUSADE. Millbrook Press.

Frost, Helen. LET'S MEET IDA B. WELLS-BARNETT. Chelsea Clubhouse Books.

McKissack, Fredrick and **Patricia**. IDA B. WELLS-BARNETT: A VOICE AGAINST VIOLENCE. Enslow Publishers.

Moore, Heidi. IDA B. WELLS-BARNETT. Heinemann Library.

Ages 9–12

McKissack, Fredrick and **Patricia.** DAYS OF JUBILEE: THE END OF SLAVERY IN THE UNITED STATES. Scholastic Press.

Medearis, Angela Shelf. THE PRINCESS OF THE PRESS: THE STORY OF IDA B. WELLS-BARNETT. Lodestar Books.

Pinkney, Andrea Davis. LET IT SHINE: STORIES OF BLACK WOMEN FREEDOM FIGHTERS. Gulliver Books/Harcourt.

Ages 13 and Up

Fradin, Dennis Brindell and **Judith Bloom Fradin**. IDA B. WELLS: MOTHER OF THE CIVIL RIGHTS MOVEMENT. Clarion Books.

Lisandrelli, Elaine Slivinski. IDA B. WELLS-BARNETT: CRUSADER AGAINST LYNCHING. Enslow Publishers.

Public Broadcasting Service (PBS) Website: The Rise and Fall of Jim Crow, Jim Crow Stories, "Ida B. Wells Forced Out of Memphis (1892)." *www.pbs.org/wnet/jimcrow/stories_events_wells.html*

Note: The quotes on pages 15, 21, 25, 28, 34, 36, and 41 were taken directly from Ida B. Wells-Barnett's writings.

Acknowledgments

I wish to extend thanks to Margaret Quinlin,
Kathy Landwehr, and Barbara Witke at Peachtree for their
encouragement and support of this project, and also to Stephen
Alcorn, whose beautifully rendered illustrations help
bring Ida's inspiring career to life.

Finally, this book would not exist at all without the
dedication and creativity of editor Emily Whitten,
who initially brought the idea to Peachtree and who was
fully a partner with the author in shaping the manuscript
for a young audience.

—*P. D.*